MW01268940

Summer

Delicious Recipes for the Warm Summer
Season

By
BookSumo Press

Published by
http://www.booksumo.com

LEGAL NOTES

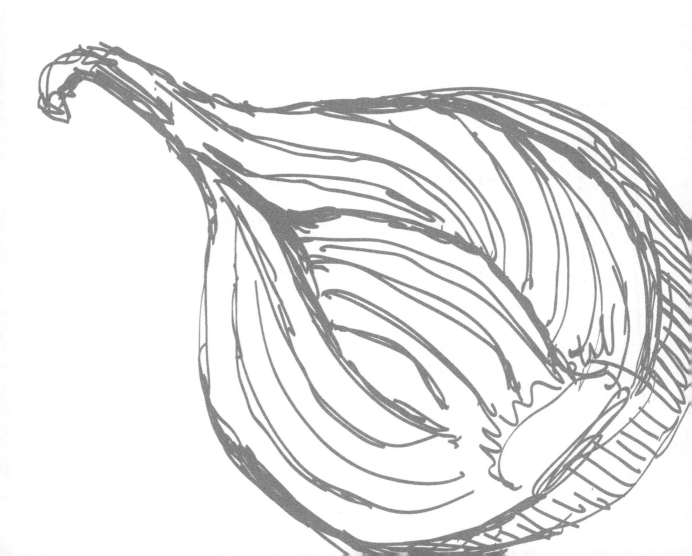

Table of Contents

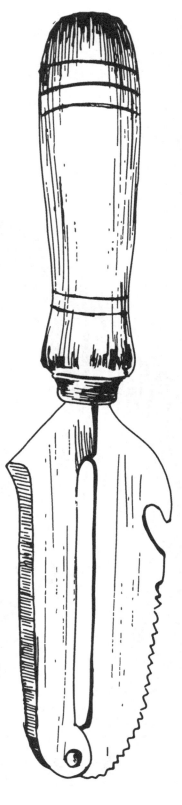

Lemonade Saint Kitts 75

Urban Garden Lemonade 76

Lebanese Lemonade 77

Black Lemonade 78

Eggs Sacramento

🥣 Prep Time: 15 mins
🕐 Total Time: 18 mins

Servings per Recipe: 24
Calories	60.1
Fat	4.6g
Cholesterol	81.8mg
Sodium	64.7mg
Carbohydrates	1.8g
Protein	3.1g

Ingredients

1 dozen egg
2 medium ripe California avocados
2 tbsps. onions, minced
1 tbsp. lemon juice
1/4 tsp. salt

1/2 tsp. paprika
6 black olives, diced

Directions

1. Place the dozen eggs in boiling water and heat for 4 minutes.
2. Remove the shells and cut the eggs into two along the length.
3. Extract the egg yolks from the whites and lay the whites on a serving dish.
4. Botch the egg yolks and avocados together.
5. Stir in the onions, salt and lemon juice.
6. Stuff the egg yolk mixture into the whites.
7. Serve sprinkled with olives and paprika.
8. Enjoy.

NEW ENGLAND
Egg Salad

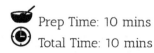 Prep Time: 10 mins

Total Time: 10 mins

Servings per Recipe: 6

Calories	178.2
Fat	8.6g
Cholesterol	240.7mg
Sodium	341.3mg
Carbohydrates	2.9g
Protein	21.9g

Ingredients

14 -15 ounces canned salmon, flaked
6 hard-boiled eggs, peeled and chopped
1/2 C. chopped onion
1/2 cucumber, peeled, seeded and chopped
1 1/2 tsps. Dijon mustard
1/2-3/4 C. mayonnaise
1/8 tsp. black pepper

1/2-3/4 tsp. dried tarragon
1/4 tsp. paprika
salt

Directions

1. Place salmon, eggs, onion, cucumber, mustard, mayonnaise, pepper, tarragon and paprika in a bowl and combine well.

2. Add salt .

3. Leave in the refrigerator to chill prior to serving.

4. Enjoy.

Blueberry
Summer Popsicles

Prep Time: 5 mins
Total Time: 2 hrs 5 mins

Servings per Recipe: 8
Calories	37 kcal
Fat	0 g
Carbohydrates	8.4g
Protein	0.9 g
Cholesterol	< 1 mg
Sodium	< 15 mg

Ingredients

1 C. Ocean Spray(R) Blueberry Juice Cocktail

1 C. Ocean Spray(R) Fresh Blueberries, cleaned and rinsed

1 (6 oz.) container fat-free vanilla yogurt

8 wooden craft sticks

Directions

1. In a blender, add all the ingredients and pulse on high speed till smooth.

2. Transfer the mixture into 8 (2.5-3 oz.)Frozen pop molds.

3. Insert the craft sticks and freeze for about 2 hours.

4. Just before serving, dip the outsides of molds into warm water to loosen.

TROPICAL
Pops

Prep Time: 15 mins
Total Time: 2 hrs 15 mins

Servings per Recipe: 6
Calories	163.9
Fat	0.4g
Cholesterol	0.0mg
Sodium	1.4mg
Carbohydrates	41.7g
Protein	0.9g

Ingredients

The pulp of 2 ripe medium-size
mangoes
3/4 C. sugar

water
3/4 C. cracked ice

Directions

1. Get a food blender: Combine in it all the ingredients. Blend them smooth.
2. Spoon the mix into 2 popsicle molds. Freeze them for 3 h.
3. Serve your popsicles.
4. Enjoy.

Bee Style
Sorbet

🥣 Prep Time: 1 hr
🕐 Total Time: 4 hrs 5 mins

Servings per Recipe: 8
Calories	188 kcal
Fat	0.1 g
Carbohydrates	50.6g
Protein	0.5 g
Cholesterol	0 mg
Sodium	3 mg

Ingredients

1 1/4 lbs Granny Smith apples, cored and thinly sliced
1 1/2 C. water
1 1/2 C. sugar

1 1/2 lemons, juiced
1 tbsp honey

Directions

1. Add your apples and some lemon juice (1/2 one lemon) to a plastic bag. Then put everything in the freezer for 8 hours.
2. Add your water and sugar to a pot and get everything boiling.
3. Set the heat to low and let the mix gently boil for 7 mins.
4. Shut the heat then combine in the honey and stir everything complete.
5. Let everything lose all its heat.
6. Add your apple to the bowl of a food processor and puree them then add in more lemon juice from 1 lemon.
7. Combine in the sugar sauce and puree everything nicely.
8. Place everything into an 8 x 8 dish then place it in the freezer for 4 hours.
9. Stir the mix every 60 mins.
10. Enjoy.

ENHANCED
Sorbet

Prep Time: 10 mins
Total Time: 20 mins

Servings per Recipe: 1
Calories	551 kcal
Fat	12.8 g
Carbohydrates	107.7g
Protein	4.3 g
Cholesterol	0 mg
Sodium	27 mg

Ingredients

1 C. preferred sorbet
2 tbsps granola, or as desired
4 strawberries, sliced
1 banana

2 tsps unsweetened coconut flakes, or as desired
1 tsp honey, or as desired

Directions

1. Add your sorbet to a bowl then add in the granola on top.
2. Layer your bananas and strawberries over the granola then layer your coconut over everything and top the dish with some honey.
3. Enjoy.

Mediterranean
Sorbet

Prep Time: 35 mins
Total Time: 1 hr 35 mins

Servings per Recipe: 4

Calories	153 kcal
Fat	0.2 g
Carbohydrates	39.6g
Protein	1.4 g
Cholesterol	0 mg
Sodium	10 mg

Ingredients

2 zucchini
1/2 C. lemon juice
1 tbsp lemon zest
2/3 C. sugar

2 sprigs mint leaves

Directions

1. Cut your zucchini into 2 pieces then throw away the seeds.
2. Slice the zucchini into bite sized pieces then place everything into the bowl food a processor and combine in the mint, lemon juice, sugar, lemon zest.
3. Puree the mix then run everything through a strainer then place a covering of plastic on the bowl and put everything in the fridge for 2 hours.
4. Place the mix into an ice cream machine and work everything into a firm smooth sorbet.
5. Enjoy.

CITRUS BOOST
Sorbet

Prep Time: 30 mins
Total Time: 1 hr 35 mins

Servings per Recipe: 10	
Calories	116 kcal
Fat	0.1 g
Carbohydrates	30.2g
Protein	0.3 g
Cholesterol	0 mg
Sodium	8 mg

Ingredients

3 large pink or red grapefruit, scrubbed
1 C. white sugar
1/4 C. light corn syrup
4 C. water

1 dash red food coloring (optional)

Directions

1. Create some long strips of zest from your grapefruits with a peeler then place the zest to the side.
2. Add the water, grapefruit zest, water, corn syrup and sugar to a pot and get everything boiling while stirring.
3. Let the mix boil for 3 mins then shut the heat and let it cool.
4. Put the pot in the fridge for faster cooling times. Then take out the zest.
5. Get a bowl for your grapefruit juice then combine the sugar sauce with the grapefruit juice then add in some food coloring to make the dish slightly pink.
6. Place everything into a bowl and put it all in the freezer for 2 hours until it is mostly frozen.
7. Once the mix is mostly frozen place everything in the food processor and puree it in batches then place everything back into the bowl and freeze it for 2 more hours.
8. Enjoy.

Old-Fashioned
American Pecan Pie

Prep Time: 10 mins
Total Time: 55 mins

Servings per Recipe: 6	
Calories	653.4
Fat	37.4
Cholesterol	120.0m
Sodium	282.6mg
Carbohydrates	78.3
Protein	6.9g

Ingredients

3 eggs
1 C. corn syrup
1 tsp vanilla extract
1 1/4 C. pecan halves

2/3 C. sugar
1/3 C. butter (melted)
1 pie crust

Directions

1. Set your oven to 350 degrees F before doing anything else.
2. In a bowl, add the eggs and beat lightly.
3. Add the corn syrup, sugar, butter and vanilla extract and stir to combine well.
4. Stir in the pecan halves and place the filling into crust.
5. Cover the edges with a piece of the foil and cook in the oven for about 25 minutes.
6. Remove the piece of foil and cook in the oven for about 20 minutes.

SUMMER
Basil Sorbet

Prep Time: 30 mins
Total Time: 2 hrs 35 mins

Servings per Recipe: 8
Calories   103 kcal
Fat   0 g
Carbohydrates   27g
Protein   0.1 g
Cholesterol   0 mg
Sodium   1 mg

Ingredients

1 C. sugar
1 C. water
3/4 C. fresh lime juice

20 fresh basil leaves, minced

Directions

1. Get your water and sugar boiling in a pot then let the mix gently cook for 2 mins.
2. Shut the heat then combine the syrup with the basil and lime juice in a food processor.
3. Puree the mix completely then enter everything into a bowl and place a covering of plastic on the bowl and put everything in the freezer for 2 hours.
4. After two hours of freezing, puree the mix in the food processor again working in batches.
5. Enjoy.

Apple Pie
from the Netherlands

Prep Time: 10 mins
Total Time: 1 hr

Servings per Recipe: 8
Calories	405.5
Fat	15.4
Cholesterol	20.3m
Sodium	189.5mg
Carbohydrates	65.8
Protein	3.2g

Ingredients

1 ready-made pie crust
5 1/2 C. peeled cored sliced cooking apples
1 tbsp lemon juice
1/2 C. granulated sugar
1/4 C. brown sugar, packed
3 tbsp flour
1/2 tsp ground cinnamon
1/4 tsp nutmeg

Topping
3/4 C. flour
1/4 C. granulated sugar
1/4 C. brown sugar, packed
1/3 C. butter, room temperature

Directions

1. Set your oven to 375 degrees F before doing anything else.
2. Arrange the pie crust into the pie plate.
3. In a large bowl, mix together the sliced apples, lemon juice, both sugars, flour, cinnamon and nutmeg.
4. Place the apple mixture into the crust.
5. For topping in a medium bowl, add the flour, both sugars and butter and with a fork, mix till a coarse crumb mixture forms.
6. Sprinkle the crumb mixture over the apples evenly.
7. Cook in the oven for about 50 minutes.

CUTE
Sorbet

Prep Time: 5 mins
Total Time: 10 mins

Servings per Recipe: 2
Calories	183 kcal
Fat	0.1 g
Carbohydrates	44.8g
Protein	0.2 g
Cholesterol	0 mg
Sodium	18 mg

Ingredients

1 C. vanilla, strawberry or raspberry sorbet, frozen yogurt or ice cream, softened
1 (8.4 oz.) can Juice Drink, any flavor, chilled

Fresh strawberry slices or raspberries, garnish

Directions

1. Separate the sorbet into serving bowls then stir each one to make it softer.
2. Add in the juice and stir everything again then top each one with some berries.
3. Enjoy.

Dreamy
Cheesy Burger

Prep Time: 15 mins
Total Time: 30 mins

Servings per Recipe: 6
Calories   466.0
Fat   24.7g
Cholesterol   102.9mg
Sodium   623.8mg
Carbohydrates   25.4g
Protein   32.8g

Ingredients

2 lbs ground beef
1 (1 oz.) package spring vegetable soup mix, like Knorr
1/2 C. minced red onion
1 1/4 C. shredded four cheese blends
6 hamburger buns split

Shredded lettuce
Sliced tomatoes
Pimento stuffed olive

Directions

1. Before you do anything preheat the grill.
2. Get a mixing bowl: Add the beef, soup mix, red onion and 1/2 C. cheese. Mix them well. Shape the mix into 6 burgers.
3. Grill the patties for 8 min on each side. Place 2 tbsps of cheese on top of each burger then cook them for 2 min until the cheese melts.
4. Assemble your burgers with lettuce and tomato slices. Serve them right away.
5. Enjoy.

PEANUT BUTTER
Burgers

Prep Time: 10 mins
Total Time: 25 mins

Servings per Recipe: 4
Calories	93.4
Fat	2.8g
Cholesterol	0.0mg
Sodium	608.6mg
Carbohydrates	13.7g
Protein	5.1g

Ingredients

1 C. textured vegetable protein
1/4 C. quick-cooking rolled oats
1/2 tsp dried oregano
1/2 tsp dried basil, flakes
1/2 tsp dried parsley flakes
1/2 tsp onion, granules
1/2 tsp garlic granules
1/4 tsp mustard powder
3/4 C. water (almost-boiling)
2 tbsps organic ketchup

2 tbsps soy sauce (or tamari or Bragg's)
1 tbsp creamy peanut butter (can also use tahini or any other nut or seed butter)
1/4 C. whole wheat pastry flour
1 tbsp nutritional yeast

Directions

1. Get a mixing bowl: Add the water with oregano, basil, parsley flakes, onion, garlic granules, and mustard powder, oats and TVP chunks. Combine them well.
2. Stir in the ketchup and soy sauce. Mix them well. Fold in the nut butter with whole-wheat pastry flour and nutritional yeast. Combine them well. Shape the mix into 4 burger cakes.
3. Place a large skillet on medium heat. Heat in it a splash of oil. Add the burgers and cook them for 7 min on each side.
4. Assemble your burgers with your favorite toppings. Serve them right away.
5. Enjoy.

Barbecue
Oat Burgers

Prep Time: 24 hrs
Total Time: 24 hrs 12 mins

Servings per Recipe: 10
Calories	219.7
Fat	13.1g
Cholesterol	63.3mg
Sodium	231.1mg
Carbohydrates	9.0g
Protein	16.0g

Ingredients

3 onions, chopped
2 tbsps minced fresh garlic
1/2 tsp cayenne pepper (or to taste)
1 tsp dried basil
1 tsp dried oregano
3 -5 tbsps olive oil
1 1/2 lbs ground turkey (use white and dark)
1/4 C. favorite barbecue sauce
3 tbsps quick-cooking oats

1/2 C. grated cheddar cheese or 1/2 C. mozzarella cheese, packed
1/3 C. grated parmesan cheese
3 tbsps milk (or use half and half cream)
2 tsps seasoning salt
1 tsp black pepper (add in more if desired)
1/3 C. dried breadcrumbs (you will most likely need more)

Directions

1. Place a large skillet on medium heat. Heat the oil in it. Add the onions with cayenne, oregano and basil. Cook them for 6 min. add the garlic and cook them for 1 min.
2. Place the mix in a mixing bowl and place it aside to lose heat. Add the turkey, BBQ sauce, oats, shredded cheese, Parmesan cheese, milk, seasoning salt, pepper. Mix them well.
3. Stir in 1/3 C. dried bread crumbs and mix them again. Add some milk if the mix is too dry. Shape the mix into 9 burgers. And wrap them in a piece of foil. Refrigerate them for 8 h.
4. Before you do anything preheat the grill.
5. Grill the burgers for 7 min on each side. Assemble with your favorite toppings. Serve your burgers right away. Enjoy.

ENSALADA
de Papas Colombiana (10-Ingredient Potato Salad)

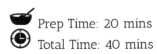 Prep Time: 20 mins
Total Time: 40 mins

Servings per Recipe: 8
Calories	124.1
Fat	2.0g
Cholesterol	0.0mg
Sodium	43.1mg
Carbohydrates	24.8g
Protein	3.1g

Ingredients

2 lb. red potatoes, cooked, peeled and cut into 1-inch cubes when cool
3 large carrots, peeled, cut into 1/2-inch pieces and steamed until crisp-tender, cooled
1/2 C. chopped red onion
1/4-1/2 C. chopped cilantro, depending on taste
3 large tomatoes, cut into 1-inch chunks

Salad Dressing
1/3 C. wine vinegar
1 tbsp oil
1 tsp seasoning salt (may add more to taste)
1 tsp sugar
1/4 tsp fresh ground black pepper

Directions

1. In a large bowl, mix together the potato cubes, carrot pieces, chopped onions and cilantro.
2. In a small bowl, add all the dressing ingredients and beat till well combined.
3. Place the dressing over the salad with the tomato chunks and gently, stir to combine.
4. Refrigerate to chill before serving.

Tuna
Salad

Prep Time: 10 mins
Total Time: 10 mins

Servings per Recipe: 4
Calories	228 kcal
Fat	17.3 g
Carbohydrates	5.3g
Protein	13.4 g
Cholesterol	24 mg
Sodium	255 mg

Ingredients

1 (7 oz.) can white tuna, drained and flaked
6 tbsps mayonnaise or salad dressing
1 tbsp Parmesan cheese
3 tbsps sweet pickle relish
1/8 tsp dried minced onion flakes

1/4 tsp curry powder
1 tbsp dried parsley
1 tsp dried dill weed
1 pinch garlic powder

Directions

1. Get a bowl, combine: onion flakes, tuna, parmesan, and mayo.
2. Stir the contents until they are smooth then add the garlic powder, curry powder, dill, and parsley.
3. Stir the contents again to evenly distribute the spices.
4. Enjoy over toasted buns or crackers.

MACARONI
Salad

Prep Time: 20 mins
Total Time: 4 hrs 30 mins

Servings per Recipe: 10
Calories	390 kcal
Fat	18.7 g
Carbohydrates	49.3g
Protein	6.8 g
Cholesterol	8 mg
Sodium	529 mg

Ingredients

4 C. uncooked elbow macaroni
1 C. mayonnaise
1/4 C. distilled white vinegar
2/3 C. white sugar
2 1/2 tbsps prepared yellow mustard
1 1/2 tsps salt
1/2 tsp ground black pepper
1 large onion, diced
2 stalks celery, diced
1 green bell pepper, seeded and diced

1/4 C. grated carrot
2 tbsps diced pimento peppers

Directions

1. Boil your macaroni in water and salt for 9 mins then remove the liquids.
2. Get a bowl, combine: macaroni, onions, pimentos, celery, carrots, black pepper, mayo, salt, green peppers, vinegar, mustard, and sugar.
3. Place a covering of plastic around the bowl and put everything in the fridge for 5 hrs.
4. Enjoy.

Indian Style
Fried Chicken

Prep Time: 15 mins

Total Time: 1 hr 15 mins

Servings per Recipe: 4

Calories	1238 kcal
Fat	96.3 g
Carbohydrates	13.8g
Protein	85.2 g
Cholesterol	1340 mg
Sodium	1430 mg

Ingredients

1 (4 lb.) whole chicken, cut into pieces
6 cloves garlic, chopped
4 tbsp oyster sauce

2 tbsp curry powder
1/2 C. vegetable oil

Directions

1. In a glass dish, mix together the oyster sauce, garlic and curry powder.
2. Add the chicken pieces and coat it with the mixture generously.
3. Cover and refrigerate for at least 1/2 hour.
4. In a large skillet, heat the oil on medium-high heat and fry the chicken pieces for about 20-25 minutes

CRISPY
Fried Chicken Croquettes

 Prep Time: 25 mins

Total Time: 2 hrs 55 mins

Servings per Recipe: 6	
Calories	377 kcal
Fat	17.5 g
Carbohydrates	26.6g
Protein	27 g
Cholesterol	137 mg
Sodium	765 mg

Ingredients

1/4 C. butter
1/4 C. flour
1/2 C. milk
1/2 C. chicken broth
3 C. finely chopped cooked chicken
1 1/2 C. seasoned bread crumbs,
divided
2 eggs, beaten
1/4 C. minced onion
1 tbsp dried parsley

1/4 tsp garlic powder
1/8 tsp celery seed
1/8 tsp cayenne pepper
salt and ground black pepper to taste
1/4 C. oil, or as needed

Directions

1. In a pan, melt the butter on medium heat.
2. Slowly, add the flour, stirring continuously and cook for about 1 minute. Slowly, add the broth and the milk, beating continuously.
3. Cook, stirring continuously for about 5-10 minute till a thick sauce forms. Remove everything from the heat and keep aside for about 10 minutes to cool. In a large bowl, add the cooled sauce, chicken, eggs, 1 C. of the breadcrumbs, onion, parsley, celery seeds, garlic powder, salt and black pepper and mix till well combined.
4. Cover and refrigerate to marinate for about 2 hours.
5. Make 6 equal sized patties from the mixture. In a shallow, dish place the remaining breadcrumbs. Roll the each patty in the breadcrumbs. In a large skillet, heat the oil on medium-high heat and cook the patties for about 5 minutes per side.
6. Transfer the chicken onto paper towel lined plates to drain.

Oriental
Fried Chicken Thighs

Prep Time: 10 mins
Total Time: 8 hrs 50 mins

Servings per Recipe: 10
Calories	877 kcal
Fat	68.5 g
Carbohydrates	120.4g
Protein	44 g
Cholesterol	222 mg
Sodium	1137 mg

Ingredients

4 eggs
1/4 C. cornstarch
1/4 C. white sugar
5 cloves garlic, minced
1/2 C. sweet rice flour
4 tsp salt

4 green onions, chopped
1/4 C. oyster sauce
5 lb. boneless chicken thighs, cut in half
2 C. vegetable oil, for deep frying

Directions

1. In a large bowl, mix together all the ingredients except the chicken and oil.
2. Add the chicken pieces and coat them with the mixture generously.
3. Cover and refrigerate everything to marinate overnight.
4. Remove the chicken pieces from the refrigerator and keep everything aside in at room temperature for about 10 minutes before cooking.
5. In a large skillet, heat the oil to 375 degrees F and fry the chicken pieces till golden brown completely.
6. Transfer the chicken pieces onto paper towel lined plates to drain.

SAN ANTONIO
Coleslaw

Prep Time: 15 mins
Total Time: 1 hr 15 mins

Servings per Recipe: 8

Calories	236 kcal
Fat	22.2 g
Carbohydrates	9.4g
Protein	2.1 g
Cholesterol	10 mg
Sodium	476 mg

Ingredients

1 C. mayonnaise
1 tbsp lime juice
1 tbsp ground cumin
1 tsp cayenne pepper
1 tsp salt
1 tsp ground black pepper
1 medium head green cabbage, rinsed
and very thinly sliced

1 large carrot, shredded
2 green onions, sliced
2 radishes, sliced

Directions

1. In a large bowl, add the mayonnaise, lime juice, cumin, salt and pepper and beat till well combined.
2. Add the cabbage, carrot, green onions and radishes and mix till well combined
3. Refrigerate to chill for at least 1 hour before serving.

Buttermilk Coleslaw

 Prep Time: 15 mins

Total Time: 1 hr 15 mins

Servings per Recipe: 8

Calories	184 kcal
Fat	12.6 g
Carbohydrates	17.1g
Protein	1.4 g
Cholesterol	11 mg
Sodium	248 mg

Ingredients

1 (16 oz.) package coleslaw mix
2 tbsp minced onion
1/3 C. white sugar
1/2 tsp salt
1/8 tsp ground black pepper
1/4 C. milk

1/2 C. mayonnaise
1/4 C. buttermilk
1 1/2 tbsp white wine vinegar
2 1/2 tbsp lemon juice

Directions

1. In a large bowl, mix together the coleslaw and onion.
2. In another bowl, add the sugar, salt, pepper, milk, mayonnaise, buttermilk, vinegar and lemon juice and mix till smooth.
3. Place the dressing over the coleslaw and onion and mix well.
4. Refrigerate to chill for at least 1 hour before serving.

AUTUMN
Picnic Coleslaw

Prep Time: 10 mins
Total Time: 1 hr 10 mins

Servings per Recipe: 8
Calories   256 kcal
Fat   23.3 g
Carbohydrates   11.4g
Protein   1.1 g
Cholesterol   15 mg
Sodium   315 mg

Ingredients

1 C. mayonnaise
2 tbsp sugar
1/2 tsp salt
1/2 tsp pepper
1/2 tsp celery seed
1/2 tsp garlic powder

1/2 tsp onion powder
2 tbsp cider vinegar
1 (16 oz.) package shredded coleslaw mix

Directions

1. In a large bowl, add the mayonnaise, sugar, salt, pepper, celery seed, garlic powder, onion powder and cider vinegar and mix well.
2. Add the coleslaw mix and toss to coat.
3. Refrigerate to chill for at least 1 hour before serving.

Elegant
Truffle Oil and Parsley Fries

🥣 Prep Time: 15 mins
🕐 Total Time: 50 mins

Servings per Recipe: 4
Calories	120 kcal
Fat	3.7 g
Carbohydrates	19.9g
Protein	2.3 g
Cholesterol	0 mg
Sodium	7 mg

Ingredients

cooking spray
1 pound potatoes, cut into strips - or more to taste
salt and ground black pepper to taste
1 tbsp white truffle oil, or to taste

2 tsps chopped fresh parsley, or more to taste

Directions

1. Coat a jelly roll pan with non-stick spray then set your oven to 350 degrees before doing anything else.

2. Layer your potato on the jelly roll pan and top them with a bit nonstick spray. Toss the potatoes then top them with some pepper and salt and toss everything again.

3. Cook the potatoes in the oven for 35 mins then let them loose their heat. Place everything into a bowl and coat the potatoes evenly with more salt, parsley, and truffle oil. Stir the potatoes to evenly coat them with oil and spice.

4. Enjoy.

SEASONED
Crinkle Cuts

Prep Time: 5 mins
Total Time: 20 mins

Servings per Recipe: 4
Calories	36.2
Fat	2.4g
Cholesterol	7.3mg
Sodium	127.3mg
Carbohydrates	0.4g
Protein	3.2g

Ingredients

5 C. frozen crinkle cut French fries
1 tsp onion salt
1/4 tsp paprika

1/3 C. grated parmesan cheese

Directions

1. Set your oven to 450 degrees before doing anything else.
2. Get a casserole dish and coat it with nonstick spray. Place your fries in the dish and top them with the paprika and onion salt.
3. Toss everything evenly to coat the fries nicely.
4. Cook your fries in the oven for about 17 mins to 22 mins or until completely done. Once the fries are finished top them with the parmesan cheese.
5. Enjoy.

How to
Bake French Fries

Prep Time: 10 mins
Total Time: 40 mins

Servings per Recipe: 4
Calories   236 kcal
Fat   8.5 g
Carbohydrates   35g
Protein   6.2 g
Cholesterol   4 mg
Sodium   1833 mg

Ingredients

cooking spray
2 large potatoes, cut into 1/4-inch slices
2 tbsps vegetable oil
1/4 C. grated Parmesan cheese
1 tbsp garlic powder

1 tbsp chopped fresh basil
1 tbsp salt
1 tbsp coarsely ground black pepper

Directions

1. Set your oven to 375 degrees before doing anything else.
2. Get a casserole dish and cover it with foil. Coat the foil with some nonstick spray then place your potatoes in a bowl.
3. Cover your potatoes with veggie oil and toss them then combine in the black pepper, parmesan, salt, basil, and garlic powder. Toss everything again to evenly coat the potatoes then layer them into the casserole dish evenly.
4. Cook everything in the oven for 31 to 36 mins or until the fries are golden.
5. Enjoy.

MANHATTAN ISLAND
Hot Dog Topping

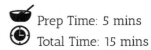 Prep Time: 5 mins
Total Time: 15 mins

Servings per Recipe: 6
Calories   166.2
Fat   8.8g
Cholesterol   50.7mg
Sodium   196.7mg
Carbohydrates   5.3g
Protein   15.9g

Ingredients

1 tsp cumin
1 C. water
1 tsp chili powder
1/2 tsp garlic powder
1 tbsp sugar
1/4 C. ketchup

1 tsp dried onion flakes
1 dash salt
1 lb hamburger

Directions

1. In a pan, add all the
2. Ingredients and cook for about 10-15 minutes.
3. Serve with the yellow mustard and onions.

Minnesota Style
Hot Dogs

Prep Time: 10 mins
Total Time: 20 mins

Servings per Recipe: 24
Calories	213.9
Fat	13.7g
Cholesterol	31.6mg
Sodium	741.9mg
Carbohydrates	15.5g
Protein	6.6g

Ingredients

1 C. cornmeal
1 3/4 C. flour
2 tsp baking powder
2 tsp salt
1 egg
1/3 C. sugar

milk
24 hot dogs
24 wooden skewers
oil

Directions

1. In a large bowl, add the cornmeal, flour, baking powder, salt, egg and sugar and mix till well combined.
2. Add the milk and mix till a mixture of pancake consistency forms.
3. With the paper towels, pat dry the hot dogs.
4. Thread the hot dogs onto floured skewers and then coat with the cornmeal mixture evenly.
5. In a deep skillet, heat about 2-inch deep oil to 370 degrees F and fry the hot dog skewers for about 2 1/2 minutes.
6. Transfer the hot dog skewers onto a paper towel lined plate to drain.
7. Drop the remaining cornmeal mixture into the oil and fry till golden brown.
8. Transfer the dumplings onto a paper towel lined plate to drain.
9. Serve the hot dog skewers alongside the ketchup and mustard tartar sauce.

HOW TO
Make An American Hot Dog

Prep Time: 5 mins
Total Time: 15 mins

Servings per Recipe: 4	
Calories	547.9
Fat	30.3g
Cholesterol	47.7mg
Sodium	1439.0mg
Carbohydrates	48.7g
Protein	18.5g

Ingredients

8 hot dogs, sliced down the middle, but not all the way through
8 buns, soft and fresh from the bakery
1 onion, chopped or sliced in rings
oil
butter, to spread on buns

Directions

1. In a non-stick pan, heat the oil on medium heat and sauté the onion till browned.
2. Transfer the onion into a bowl and cover with a piece of foil to keep warm.
3. In the same pan, place the hot dogs, cut side down and cook till browned from both sides.
4. Transfer the hot dog into a bowl.
5. Split open the buns and spread the butter on them.
6. In the same pan, place the buttered buns, face down on medium heat and toast till nicely browned.
7. Transfer the toasted buns onto a plate.
8. Arrange the hot dog and cooked onions over the bun.
9. Top with the mustard and ketchup and serve.

Tandoori
Apple Asiago Sandwich

🥘 Prep Time: 15 mins
🕐 Total Time: 30 mins

Servings per Recipe: 3
Calories	342 kcal
Fat	21.9 g
Carbohydrates	30.5g
Protein	9.5 g
Cholesterol	26 mg
Sodium	492 mg

Ingredients

1 apple, cored and chopped
1/3 bunch kale, chopped
1 tbsp tandoori seasoning
1 tsp cayenne pepper
1/4 C. apple cider
1 tbsp olive oil

4 slices bacon
3 large cracked wheat dinner-style rolls, split
3 tbsps grated Asiago cheese

Directions

1. Fry your bacon for 11 mins then place the bacon on some paper towel to drain.
2. Begin to stir the following in the apple cider, apples, cayenne, kale, and tandoori spice.
3. Top the mix with the olive oil as it fries in the bacon fat and let everything cook for 8 mins. Then place the mix to the side.
4. Evenly coat the bottom piece of the bread with the tandoori mix then with some bacon and asiago.
5. Form sandwiches with the other half of the bread.
6. Enjoy.

CRAB
Salad Sandwich

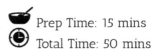

Prep Time: 15 mins
Total Time: 50 mins

Servings per Recipe: 2
Calories	478 kcal
Fat	30 g
Carbohydrates	39.7g
Protein	13 g
Cholesterol	48 mg
Sodium	1413 mg

Ingredients

1 (8 oz.) package imitation crab or
lobster meat
1/4 C. mayonnaise
1 tbsp finely chopped red onion
1 tsp lemon juice
1/4 tsp seafood Seasoning

1 tbsp butter, softened
2 hot dog buns

Directions

1. Get a bowl, combine: seafood seasoning, crab (flaked), lemon juice, mayo, and onions.
2. Place a covering of plastic around the bowl and put everything in the oven for 35 mins.
3. Now get your oven's broiler hot before continuing
4. Place your buns in a broiler pan after coating them with the butter.
5. Broil the bread until it is nicely toasted for a few mins then top each one evenly with the crab salad.
6. Enjoy.

Tuna
Sandwiches

🍲 Prep Time: 15 mins
🕐 Total Time: 15 mins

Servings per Recipe: 2
Calories   553 kcal
Fat   32.9 g
Carbohydrates   30.2g
Protein   33.7 g
Cholesterol   63 mg
Sodium   656 mg

Ingredients

1 (6 oz.) can tuna, drained
1/4 C. mayonnaise
1 1/2 tsps cream-style horseradish sauce
1 tbsp chopped dill pickles
2 leaves lettuce
2 slices Swiss cheese

4 slices bread
2 slices tomato
2 thin slices red onion

Directions

1. Get a bowl, combine: pickles, tuna, horseradish, and mayo. Stir the mix until it even and smooth.
2. Top 2 pieces of bread with 1 piece of Swiss and a piece of lettuce. Evenly divide your tuna mix between the bread slices then layer your onions and tomatoes.
3. Place the other piece of bread to make a sandwich.
4. Enjoy.

BLUEBERRY
Muffins

Prep Time: 10 mins
Total Time: 50 mins

Servings per Recipe: 18
Calories	182 kcal
Fat	5.9 g
Carbohydrates	30.5g
Protein	2.4 g
Cholesterol	34 mg
Sodium	165 mg

Ingredients

2 C. all-purpose flour
2 tsps baking powder
Salt, to taste
1 1/2 C. white sugar, divided
1/2 C. butter, softened
2 eggs

1/4 C. milk
1/2 C. fresh blueberries, mashed
2 C. fresh blueberries

Directions

1. Set your oven to 375 degrees before doing anything else.
2. Grease and flour an 18 C. muffin tin.
3. In a large bowl, mix together the flour, baking powder and salt.
4. In another bowl, add 1 1/4 C. of sugar and butter and beat till light.
5. Add the eggs, one at a time and beat till well combined.
6. Add the egg mixture into the flour mixture and mix till well combined.
7. Add the milk and mix well.
8. Add the mashed blueberries and mix well.
9. Fold in the fresh blueberries.
10. Place the mixture into prepared muffin C. so that about 2/3 of each section is full.
11. Dust with the remaining sugar.
12. Bake everything for about 30 minutes or till a toothpick inserted in the center comes out clean.

Honey
Spelt Bread

Prep Time: 10 mins

Total Time: 1 hr 30 mins

Servings per Recipe: 12

Calories	118 kcal
Fat	1.3 g
Carbohydrates	23g
Protein	4.9 g
Cholesterol	1 mg
Sodium	302 mg

Ingredients

1 C. water
1 1/2 tsp vegetable oil
1 1/2 tsp honey
1/2 tsp lecithin
3 C. white spelt flour
3 tbsp dry milk powder

1 1/2 tsp salt
2 tsp active dry yeast

Directions

1. In the bread machine pan, place all the ingredients in the order recommended by the manufacturer.
2. Set the Normal or Basic cycle and press Start

PICNIC
Pumpernickel Bread

Prep Time: 10 mins
Total Time: 3 hrs 55 mins

Servings per Recipe: 12

Calories	181 kcal
Fat	2.6 g
Carbohydrates	34.8g
Protein	5.5 g
Cholesterol	0 mg
Sodium	296 mg

Ingredients

1 1/8 C. warm water
1 1/2 tbsp vegetable oil
1/3 C. molasses
3 tbsp cocoa
1 tbsp caraway seed (optional)
1 1/2 tsp salt

1 1/2 C. bread flour
1 C. rye flour
1 C. whole wheat flour
1 1/2 tbsp vital wheat gluten (optional)
2 1/2 tsp bread machine yeast

Directions

1. In the bread machine pan, place all the ingredients in the order recommended by the manufacturer.
2. Set the Basic cycle and press Start.

Bruschetta
Summers

Prep Time: 5 mins
Total Time: 6 mins

Servings per Recipe: 5

Calories	728.3
Fat	18.2 g
Cholesterol	0.0 mg
Sodium	1053.1 mg
Carbohydrates	117.5 g
Protein	24.4 g

Ingredients

1 loaf crusty bread, sliced into 10 slices
2 garlic cloves, minced
1/3 C. olive oil
3 plum tomatoes, diced
1 tsp diced onion
2 tsp chopped fresh basil

salt & pepper
1/2 tsp balsamic vinegar

Directions

1. Set your grill for high heat and lightly, grease the grill grate.
2. In a bowl, add the garlic and oil and mix well.
3. Keep aside for about 10 minutes.
4. Coat the both sides of each bread slice with a thin layer of the oil.
5. Cook the bread slices onto the grill until toasted.
6. Meanwhile, in the bowl of remaining garlic oil, add the onion, tomatoes, herbs, vinegar, salt and pepper and mix well.
7. Place the tomato mixture over each slice and enjoy.

HOW TO
Grill Corn

Prep Time: 35 mins
Total Time: 1 hr 5 mins

Servings per Recipe: 4
Calories	77.4
Fat	1.0 g
Cholesterol	0.0 mg
Sodium	13.5 mg
Carbohydrates	17.1 g
Protein	2.9 g

Ingredients

4 ears sweet corn
ice cold water

Directions

1. Carefully, pull the husks of each kernel back to within 2-inch of the base.
2. Carefully, remove the silk and then, smooth husks back into place, covering the kernels completely.
3. In a bowl of ice water, place the corn and keep aside for about 30 minutes.
4. Drain the corn completely and shake off the excess water.
5. Set your grill for medium-high heat and generously, grease the grill grate.
6. Place the corn onto the grill over coals 5-inches from the heat and cook for about 15 minutes, flipping often.
7. Enjoy warm.

Alabama
Yams

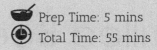

Prep Time: 5 mins
Total Time: 55 mins

Servings per Recipe: 2
Calories	127.8
Fat	5.7 g
Cholesterol	15.2 mg
Sodium	76.9 mg
Carbohydrates	18.7 g
Protein	1.1 g

Ingredients

1 large sweet potato, halved lengthwise
1 tbsp butter, softened
salt
pepper

2 tsp honey

Directions

1. Set your grill for medium-high heat.
2. Arrange each potato half onto of an 18x12-inch piece of foil.
3. Place the butter onto the cut side of each potato half and season with the salt and pepper.
4. Fold each foil piece over potatoes tightly to seal.
5. Place the foil packet onto the grill and cook, covered for about 50 minutes, flipping once half way through.
6. Remove from the grill and carefully, open each foil packet.
7. With a fork, fluff the potatoes and enjoy with a topping of the honey.

JIMMY'S
Grilled Beef

Prep Time: 45 mins
Total Time: 48 hrs 45 mins

Servings per Recipe: 8

Calories	307.7
Fat	31.0 g
Cholesterol	17.4 mg
Sodium	38.3 mg
Carbohydrates	4.2 g
Protein	4.7 g

Ingredients

1 beef tenderloin
1 C. olive oil
1/2 C. fresh thyme, chopped
1/2 C. fresh rosemary, chopped
4 cloves garlic
1/4 C. fresh cracked black pepper
soaked hickory chips

Sauce
1 C. mayonnaise
6 tsp horseradish
2 tsp Dijon mustard
2 tsp lemon juice
salt and pepper

Directions

1. In a blender, add the oil, garlic, fresh herbs and black pepper and pulse until smooth. Coat the tenderloin with the mixture evenly.
2. With a plastic wrap, wrap the tenderloin and place in the fridge for about 48 hours. For the sauce: in a bowl, add all the ingredients and mix until well combined.
3. Refrigerate to chill for the whole day.
4. Remove the tenderloin from the fridge and keep side in room temperature for about 2 hours before grilling.
5. Set your grill for medium-high heat and grease the grill grate.
6. Season the tenderloin with the salt evenly.
7. Place a pan of the soaked hickory chips onto a lower rack.
8. Now, set the grill to medium heat.
9. Place the tenderloin onto a rack over the chips and cook for about 45-60 minutes.
10. Enjoy the tenderloin alongside the sauce.

Kerala
Chicken

🥣 Prep Time: 5 mins
🕐 Total Time: 17 mins

Servings per Recipe: 4
Calories   237.6
Fat   10.3 g
Cholesterol   75.5 mg
Sodium   804.6 mg
Carbohydrates   10.3 g
Protein   25.6 g

Ingredients

2 tbsp vegetable oil
2 tbsp grainy mustard
2 tbsp liquid honey
2 tsp curry powder
1 tsp salt
1/2 tsp garlic powder
1/2 tsp ground black pepper

1/2 tsp cinnamon
4 boneless skinless chicken breasts
1/4 C. chopped coriander

Directions

1. Set your BBQ grill for medium heat and grease the grill grate.
2. In a bowl, add the oil, honey, mustard, curry powder, cinnamon, garlic powder, salt and pepper and mix until well combined.
3. Coat the chicken with the mixture generously.
4. Cook the chicken onto the grill for about 10 minutes, flipping and coating with the remaining marinade often.
5. Enjoy with a garnishing of the coriander.

COOKOUT
Pizza

Prep Time: 15 mins
Total Time: 30 mins

Servings per Recipe: 12	
Calories	162.1
Fat	18.0 g
Cholesterol	0.0 mg
Sodium	97.7 mg
Carbohydrates	0.6 g
Protein	0.1 g

Ingredients

1 (1 lb.) package frozen bread dough
Garnish
turkey bacon, chopped
sliced tomatoes
fresh asparagus
shaved Parmesan cheese
onion
herbs
Spice Mix
1 C. extra virgin olive oil
2 tsp ground oregano
1 tsp onion powder
3/4 tsp ground black pepper
1/2 tsp curry powder
1/2 tsp salt
1/2 tsp garlic powder
1/2 tsp red pepper flakes
1/4 tsp ground cumin
1/4 tsp cayenne pepper
chopped tomato
chopped onion
chopped basil

Directions

1. For the seasoning: in a pot, add all the ingredients over low heat and cook until just warmed, beating continuously.

2. Remove from the heat and keep aside in room temperature for about 2 hours. Set your grill for medium heat and lightly, grease the grill grate. For the pizza bread: lightly flour the back of a 15x10-inch baking sheet. With your hands, stretch the dough into the size to fit onto the baking sheet. Arrange the stretched dough onto the back of the baking sheet. Coat the surface of the dough with the seasoned oil evenly.

3. Carefully, flip the baking sheet onto the grill grate over direct heat and remove the baking sheet. Coat the top side of the dough with the seasoned oil generously. Cook for about 1-3 minutes.

4. Carefully, flip the side of dough and coat the top with the seasoned oil. Cook for about 3-4 minutes. Remove the crust from the grill and keep aside onto a wire rack to cool slightly. Arrange your desired topping over the crust. Place the pizza onto the grill and cook, covered until the doneness of your liking. Repeat with the remaining 2 dough balls. Enjoy hot.

Sweet and Sour Grilled Fish

🥣 Prep Time: 5 mins
🕐 Total Time: 15 mins

Servings per Recipe: 2
Calories   418.0
Fat   23.2 g
Cholesterol   93.5 mg
Sodium   230.7 mg
Carbohydrates   15.4 g
Protein   35.3 g

Ingredients

1 1/2 tbsp honey
1 1/2 tbsp Dijon mustard
1 tbsp balsamic vinegar
1/4 tsp ground pepper

1/4 tsp garlic salt
2 (6 oz.) salmon steaks
cooking spray

Directions

1. Set your grill for medium-high heat and grease the grill grate.
2. In a bowl, add all the ingredients except the salmon steaks and mix until well combined.
3. Add the salmon steaks and coat with the mixture generously.
4. Place the salmon steaks onto the grill and cook, covered for about 4-6 minutes, flipping once half way through.
5. Enjoy hot.

HOT
Tropical Glazed Chicken Cutlets

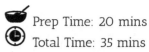

Prep Time: 20 mins
Total Time: 35 mins

Servings per Recipe: 8
Calories	229.0
Fat	10.3 g
Cholesterol	46.4 mg
Sodium	69.6 mg
Carbohydrates	18.7 g
Protein	16.5 g

Ingredients

Chicken
4 large boneless chicken breasts
Marinade
2 tbsp minced garlic
2 tbsp fresh minced thyme
2 tbsp extra virgin olive oil
1 tbsp black pepper
pineapple juice
1 pinch salt
Salsa
1 chipotle chile, seeded & chopped
1 small red pepper, diced

1 garlic, minced
1/2 C. fresh cilantro, chopped
1/2 vidalia onion, chopped
1 (15 oz.) cans crushed pineapple, drained
1 mango, diced
2 tbsp lime juice
1 tsp grated fresh ginger
salt

Directions

1. For the salsa: in a bowl, add all the ingredients and mix well.
2. Refrigerate to chill before using. In a re-sealable bag, add all the marinade ingredients and chicken breasts.
3. Seal the bag and shake to coat well.
4. Refrigerate for about 45 minutes. Set your grill for high heat and grease the grill grate. Place the chicken breasts onto the grill, skin side and immediately, set the grill to medium.
5. Cook them onto the grill for about 10 minutes, flipping once half way through. Now, set the grill to medium-low and cook for about 5 minutes. Enjoy the chicken hot alongside the salsa.

Hot
Glazed Fish Filets

🥣 Prep Time: 20 mins
🕐 Total Time: 30 mins

Servings per Recipe: 4
Calories	281.8
Fat	4.2 g
Cholesterol	144.7 mg
Sodium	2557.2 mg
Carbohydrates	24.6 g
Protein	38.6 g

Ingredients

Fish
4 (7 oz.) mahi mahi fillets
1 tbsp kosher salt
2 tbsp cracked black pepper
Salsa
2 C. mangoes, peeled and cubed
1/2 C. sweet kernel corn
1/2 lime, juiced
1/2 lemon, juiced
1/2 C. grape tomatoes, quartered

2 tsp olive oil
1 habanero pepper, seeded and chopped
1/4 C. chopped cilantro
1 tsp salt
1 tsp pepper

Directions

1. For the salsa: in a bowl, add all the ingredients except the mango and mix well.
2. Cover the bowl and place in the fridge for all the night.
3. Set your grill for medium heat and grease the grill grate.
4. Cook the Mahi Mahi fillets onto the grill for about 10 minutes, flipping once half way through.
5. Remove from the grill and sprinkle each fillet with the salt and pepper evenly.
6. In the bowl of the salsa, add the mango and gently, stir to combine.
7. Enjoy the Mahi Mahi fillets alongside the salsa.

CAROLINA
Country Catfish

Prep Time: 10 mins
Total Time: 20 mins

Servings per Recipe: 4
Calories   246.0
Fat   13.7 g
Cholesterol   79.9 mg
Sodium   1274.3 mg
Carbohydrates   2.9 g
Protein   27.1 g

Ingredients

3 tsp paprika
3 tsp chili powder
1 -1 1/2 tsp ground cumin
1 -1 1/2 tsp ground coriander
1 tsp cayenne pepper
1/2 tsp garlic powder

2 tsp salt
4 (6 oz.) catfish fillets

Directions

1. Set your grill for medium heat and grease the grill grate.
2. In a bowl, add all the ingredients except the catfish fillets and mix until well combined.
3. Add the catfish fillets and coat with the spice mixture generously.
4. Cook the catfish fillets onto the grill for about 10 minutes, flipping once half way through.
5. Enjoy hot.

Grilled
Seattle Flatbreads

🥣 Prep Time: 10 mins
🕐 Total Time: 25 mins

Servings per Recipe: 4
Calories	305.9
Fat	14.4 g
Cholesterol	44.8 mg
Sodium	614.3 mg
Carbohydrates	26.9 g
Protein	16.6 g

Ingredients

4 slices eggplants
extra virgin olive oil
salt, pepper
8 slices country bread

2 C. arugula leaves
8 oz. sliced mozzarella cheese

Directions

1. Coat the eggplant slices with the oil evenly.
2. Place the eggplant slices in a George Foreman grill and cook for about 4 minutes.
3. Transfer the eggplant slices onto a plate.
4. Now, coat one side of each bread slice with the oil evenly.
5. Place 4 bread slices onto a platter, oiled side down and top each with the eggplant, followed by the arugula and mozzarella cheese.
6. Cover each with the remaining 4 bread slices, oiled side up.
7. Place 2 sandwiches on a hot grill and cook, covered for about 3-4 minutes.
8. Repeat with the remaining sandwiches.
9. Cut each sandwich in half diagonally and enjoy.

BROCCOLI
on the Grill

Prep Time: 10 mins
Total Time: 50 mins

Servings per Recipe: 6	
Calories	126.2
Fat	8.4 g
Cholesterol	11.0 mg
Sodium	318.2 mg
Carbohydrates	7.0 g
Protein	7.4 g

Ingredients

6 C. fresh broccoli stems
2 1/2 tbsp lemon juice
2 tbsp olive oil
1/4 tsp salt

1/4 tsp pepper
3/4 C. grated Parmesan cheese

Directions

1. In a bowl, add the oil, lemon juice, salt and pepper and mix well.
2. Add the broccoli and toss to coat well.
3. Keep aside for about 30 minutes.
4. Set your grill for medium heat and grease the grill grate.
5. Toss the broccoli again and remove from the bowl, discarding the marinade.
6. In a re-sealable bag, add the Parmesan and broccoli.
7. Seal the bag and shake well to coat.
8. Place the broccoli onto the grill over indirect heat and cook, covered for about 16 - 20 minutes, flipping once half way through.
9. Enjoy warm.

How to
Grill Tofu Asian Street Style

🥣 Prep Time: 10 mins
🕐 Total Time: 20 mins

Servings per Recipe: 1
Calories   278.0
Fat   1.6g
Cholesterol   0.0mg
Sodium   5992.4mg
Carbohydrates   65.2g
Protein   7.8g

Ingredients

2 pieces firm tofu
1 large green mango, peeled and shredded
1 tsp soy sauce
1 dash black pepper

1/4 C. fish sauce

Directions

1. Set your grill for medium heat and lightly, grease the grill grate.
2. Coat the tofu with the soy sauce evenly and then, season with the black pepper.
3. Cook the tofu onto grill until golden brown from both sides.
4. Place the mango onto a serving platter and top with the tofu.
5. Enjoy.

HOT
Beef Kabobs

Prep Time: 20 mins
Total Time: 40 mins

Servings per Recipe: 4	
Calories	308.9
Fat	20.4g
Cholesterol	0.4mg
Sodium	2080.4mg
Carbohydrates	25.2g
Protein	10.4g

Ingredients

24 oz. dry-aged boneless beef
tenderloin, cut into strips
2 garlic cloves, minced
2 stalks lemongrass
1 tbsp coriander seed
2 tbsp brown sugar
1/4 C. fish sauce
1/4 C. dry roasted peanuts, crushed
Peanut Sauce
1/4 C. roasted peanuts, ground
1 tbsp peanut oil

2 garlic cloves, minced
2 tsp chili paste
2 tbsp tomato paste
1/2 C. chicken broth
1/2 tsp sugar
1 tbsp peanut butter
1/4 C. hoisin sauce
1 red chili, seeded and sliced

Directions

1. In a food processor, add the lemon grass, garlic, sugar, coriander and fish sauce and pulse until a smooth paste is formed.
2. In a bowl, add the meat and marinade and mix well.
3. Refrigerate for about 16-24 hours. For the peanut sauce: in a pot, add the oil and cook until heated through.
4. Add the garlic, tomato paste and chili paste and sauté for about 1-2 minutes. Add the peanut butter, sugar, hoisin sauce and broth and cook for about 4 minutes. Remove from the heat and keep aside to cool.
5. Stir in the peanuts and chilies and keep aside. Set your grill for high heat and lightly, grease the grill grate. Thread the beef onto skewers. Place the skewers onto the grill over direct heat and cook until desired doneness.
6. Enjoy with a garnishing of the roasted peanuts alongside the sauce.

Tropical
Teriyaki Kabobs

Prep Time: 15 mins
Total Time: 20 mins

Servings per Recipe: 4
Calories	931.9
Fat	82.8g
Cholesterol	112.3mg
Sodium	2046.7mg
Carbohydrates	34.4g
Protein	13.8g

Ingredients

- 1 lb. beef, cubed
- 1 (16 ounce) cans pineapple chunks in juice
- 1/2 C. soy sauce
- 1/4 C. brown sugar
- 2 garlic cloves, minced
- 1/2 tsp minced ginger
- 1/2 tsp sliced lemongrass
- 1/4 C. sliced scallion
- 2 tsps sesame oil

Directions

1. Get a large zip lock bag: Place in it all the ingredients and seal it.
2. Shake it to coat them. Place it in the fridge for 3 h.
3. Before you do anything, preheat the grill and grease it.
4. Drain the beef and pineapple chunks from the marinade. Thread them while alternating between them onto skewers.
5. Grill them for 4 to 6 min on each side. Serve them warm.
6. Enjoy.

TEXAS
Potatoes

Prep Time: 5 mins
Total Time: 1 hr 5 mins

Servings per Recipe: 1
Calories   741.4
Fat   50.4 g
Cholesterol   61.0 mg
Sodium   226.9 mg
Carbohydrates   67.9 g
Protein   8.1 g

Ingredients

1 large potato
1/4 large Spanish onion, cut into 4 slices
2 - 3 tbsp butter
2 - 3 tbsp olive oil

salt & fresh ground pepper
aluminum foil

Directions

1. Set your BBQ grill for medium heat and lightly, grease the grill grate.
2. Scrub the potato and then, make 4 slits almost through to bottom.
3. Insert 1 onion slice into each potato slit.
4. Place the butter on top of the potato in the form of the butter.
5. Season with the salt and pepper and drizzle with the oil.
6. With a piece of the foil, wrap the potato tightly.
7. Place the foil parcel onto the rack and cook, covered for about 1 hour.
8. Enjoy warm.

My First
Beef Brisket

🥣 Prep Time: 15 mins
🕐 Total Time: 48 hrs 15 mins

Servings per Recipe: 12
Calories   511.7
Fat   23.3 g
Cholesterol   187.4 mg
Sodium   3407.4 mg
Carbohydrates   9.1 g
Protein   63.8 g

Ingredients

1 (8 -14 lb.) beef brisket, trimmed
1/4 C. paprika
1/3 C. kosher salt
2 tbsp sugar
2 tbsp brown sugar
3 tbsp cumin

2 tbsp chili powder
2 tbsp ground pepper
2 tbsp cayenne
1 tbsp onion powder
1 tbsp garlic powder

Directions

1. In a bowl, add all the ingredients except the brisket and mix until well combined.
2. Rub the both sides of the brisket with the spice mixture generously.
3. With a few layers of the plastic wrap, wrap the brisket tightly.
4. Then, with a piece of the foil wrap the brisket and refrigerate for all the day.
5. Set your smoker to 225-240 degrees F, using the pecan wood chips.
6. Place the brisket in the smoker and cook for about 1 1/2 hours per pound, adding some soaked chips after every 30 minutes in first 8 hours of the cooking.
7. Remove from the smoker and with a piece of the foil, wrap the brisket for about 30 minutes before slicing.
8. Cut the brisket into slices against the grain and enjoy.

CRUSTED
Grilled Salmon

Prep Time: 20 mins
Total Time: 40 mins

Servings per Recipe: 8
Calories	264.4
Fat	10.9 g
Cholesterol	77.4 mg
Sodium	129.6 mg
Carbohydrates	5.3 g
Protein	35.3 g

Ingredients

8 (6 oz.) salmon fillets, skinless
2 cedar planks, soaked in water for 4 to
6 hours
1 tbsp dry barbecue spice
sea salt
1 large lemon
Crust
1 C. fresh dill, chopped

1/2 C. shallot, chopped
2 garlic cloves, chopped
2 green onions, chopped
3 tbsp cracked black pepper
2 tbsp olive oil
1 lemon, juice

Directions

1. Set your grill for high heat and grease the grill grate.
2. Season the salmon fillets with the BBQ seasoning evenly.
3. For the crust: in a bowl, add all the ingredients and mix well.
4. Coat the flesh side of the salmon fillets with the crust mixture generously.
5. Sprinkle the soaked cedar planks with the salt, and place onto the grill.
6. Close lid of the grill and heat for about 3-5 minutes.
7. Arrange the salmon fillets on hot planks, skinned side down and cook, covered for about 12-15 minutes.
8. Enjoy with a drizzling of the lemon juice.

Summer
Teriyaki BBQ

Prep Time: 15 mins
Total Time: 40 mins

Servings per Recipe: 2
Calories	264.1
Fat	2.2g
Cholesterol	68.4mg
Sodium	1475.6mg
Carbohydrates	27.5g
Protein	36.1g

Ingredients

2 boneless skinless chicken breast halves
1 small zucchini, cut into bite-size pieces
1 large green pepper, cut into chunks
2 small onions, quartered, each quarter cut in half
8 ounces mushrooms, halved
10 cloves garlic
1/4-1/2 C. teriyaki marinade

salt and pepper
garlic powder
5 -6 Bbq skewers

Directions

1. Thread the veggies onto skewers while alternating between them.
2. Make 5 slits in each chicken breast. Press a clove of garlic into each slit.
3. Season them with some garlic powder, salt and pepper then coat them with the teriyaki sauce.
4. Before you do anything, preheat the grill and grease its grates with oil.
5. Arrange over it the chicken breasts and veggies skewers.
6. Cook them for 5 to 8 min on each side until they are done.
7. Serve your grill chicken and veggies warm.
8. Enjoy.

HOW TO
Make Ribs

Prep Time: 30 mins
Total Time: 6 hrs 30 mins

Servings per Recipe: 4
Calories   349.8
Fat   12.6 g
Cholesterol   0.0 mg
Sodium   1352.1 mg
Carbohydrates   69.2 g
Protein   13.1 g

Ingredients

brown sugar
honey
dry rub seasonings
1/3 C. brown sugar
11 oz. chili powder
2 tbsp seasoning salt
2 tbsp garlic powder

2 tbsp onion powder
2 tbsp cayenne
1 tbsp cracked black pepper
2 tbsp paprika
ribs

Directions

1. Preheat the smoker to 250-275 degrees F, using pecan or apple wood chips.
2. Coat the ribs with the dry rub and keep aside for about 1 hour.
3. Place the ribs over indirect heat and cook for about 2 1/2 hours.
4. Now, coat the meat with the brown sugar and honey generously.
5. With foil pieces, cover the ribs.
6. Cook for about 2 1/2-3 hours.
7. Enjoy hot.

Asian
Backyard Beef

🥣 Prep Time: 15 mins
🕐 Total Time: 25 mins

Servings per Recipe: 6
Calories   507.4
Fat   33.5 g
Cholesterol   128.5 mg
Sodium   1419.1 mg
Carbohydrates   15.6 g
Protein   33.2 g

Ingredients

2 lb. beef boneless sirloin, sliced across the grain
1/2 C. soy sauce
1/3 C. sugar
3 tbsp sake
2 tbsp dark sesame oil
8 garlic cloves, sliced

4 scallions, both white and green parts, trimmed and minced
2 tbsp sesame seeds, toasted
1/2 tsp ground black pepper

Directions

1. Arrange the beef slices between 2 plastic wrap sheets with a rolling pin, pound into a 1/8-inch thickness.
2. In a bowl, add all the ingredients and beat until well combined.
3. Add the beef slices and coat with the marinade generously.
4. Cover the baking dish and place in the fridge for about 2 hours.
5. Set your grill for high heat and grease the grill grate.
6. Cook the beef slices onto the grill for about 2-4 minutes, flipping once half way through.
7. Enjoy hot.

TAMPA
Scallops

Prep Time: 5 mins
Total Time: 17 mins

Servings per Recipe: 2
Calories	390.2
Fat	24.5 g
Cholesterol	115.5 mg
Sodium	1104.0 mg
Carbohydrates	11.9 g
Protein	31.4 g

Ingredients

1 lb. scallops
8 oz. mushrooms, sliced
1/4 C. butter, sliced
4 tbsp parsley, minced

1 - 2 clove garlic, minced
1 tsp lemon pepper seasoning

Directions

1. Set your grill for medium-low heat.
2. Place the scallops onto a piece of the foil, followed by the mushrooms, butter, parsley and garlic.
3. Sprinkle with the lemon pepper seasoning evenly.
4. Fold the foil tightly to seal.
5. Place the foil parcel onto the grill and cook for about 12 minutes.
6. Enjoy warm.

Glazed
Dijon Salmon

🥘 Prep Time: 5 mins
🕐 Total Time: 20 mins

Servings per Recipe: 4
Calories	435.6
Fat	15.0 g
Cholesterol	78.4 mg
Sodium	3589.9 mg
Carbohydrates	32.2 g
Protein	46.1 g

Ingredients

1/3 C. orange juice
1/3 C. soy sauce
1/4 C. honey
1 tbsp Dijon mustard
1 inch ginger, chopped

2 garlic cloves, minced
3 green onions, chopped
1 1/2 lb. salmon fillets

Directions

1. In a bowl, add all the ingredients except the salmon fillets and mix until well combined.
2. Add the salmon fillets and coat with the marinade generously.
3. Place in the fridge for about 20-25 minutes.
4. Set your grill for medium-high heat and grease the grill grate.
5. Cook the salmon fillets onto the grill for about 10-12 minutes, flipping once half way through.
6. Enjoy hot.

GRILLED
Chicken with Tang

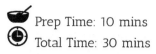

Prep Time: 10 mins
Total Time: 30 mins

Servings per Recipe: 4
Calories	406.2
Fat	22.5 g
Cholesterol	188.4 mg
Sodium	525.1 mg
Carbohydrates	2.4 g
Protein	44.9 g

Ingredients

1/2 C. cider vinegar
1/4 C. oil
3/4 tsp kosher salt
1/4 C. shallot

2 garlic cloves, chopped
2 lb. skinless chicken thighs, trimmed of fat

Directions

1. In a bowl, add all the ingredients except the chicken thighs and mix until well combined.
2. Add the chicken thighs and coat with the marinade generously.
3. Place in the fridge for about 2-3 hours.
4. Set your grill for medium heat and grease the grill grate.
5. Cook them onto the grill for about 4 minutes per side.
6. Cook the chicken thighs onto the grill for about 12-16 minutes, flipping once half way through.
7. Enjoy hot.

Dads'
Steak Recipe

Prep Time: 15 mins
Total Time: 27 mins

Servings per Recipe: 4
Calories   145.5
Fat   14.7 g
Cholesterol   38.9 mg
Sodium   258.6 mg
Carbohydrates   1.1 g
Protein   2.6 g

Ingredients

Butter
2 garlic cloves, chopped
1/4 tsp onion powder
1/4 tsp McCormick's Montreal Brand steak seasoning
1/4 C. butter
1/3 C. crumbled blue cheese
1/4 tsp dried thyme

Steak
4 petite fillets mignon steaks
3 - 4 cloves garlic, chopped
1/4 tsp seasoning salt
1/4 black pepper
1/4 soy sauce
cooking spray

Directions

1. For the garlic butter: in a blender, add all the ingredients except the blue cheese and pulse until well combined.
2. Add the blue cheese and pulse until pureed.
3. Transfer into a bowl and place in the fridge until using.
4. For the steaks: in a bowl, add the soy sauce, garlic, seasoned salt and pepper and mix well.
5. Add the steaks and coat with the marinade generously.
6. Place in the fridge for about 15 minutes, flipping once.
7. Set your grill for medium heat and grease the grill grate.
8. Cook them onto the grill for about 12 minutes, flipping once half way through.
9. Enjoy the steaks with a topping of the garlic butter.

GREEN BEAN
Griller

Prep Time: 15 mins
Total Time: 35 mins

Servings per Recipe: 8
Calories	58.7
Fat	1.9 g
Cholesterol	0.0 mg
Sodium	73.6 mg
Carbohydrates	9.8 g
Protein	2.2 g

Ingredients

1 tbsp brown sugar
1 tbsp sesame oil
1 tbsp reduced sodium soy sauce
2 garlic cloves, minced
1/2 tsp crushed red pepper flakes

1 1/2 lb. green beans, trimmed
1 medium red onion, halved and sliced
6 medium mushrooms, quartered

Directions

1. Set your grill for medium heat.
2. In a bowl, add the brown sugar, sesame oil, soy sauce, garlic and red pepper flakes and mix until well combined.
3. Add the green beans, mushrooms and onion and toss to combine.
4. Divide the veggie mixture onto 2 (18-inch square) foil pieces evenly.
5. Fold foil around vegetables tightly to seal completely.
6. Place the foil parcels onto the grill and cook, covered for about 18-22 minutes, flipping the parcels occasionally.
7. Enjoy warm.

Garden
Fish Filets

Prep Time: 15 mins
Total Time: 25 mins

Servings per Recipe: 4
Calories   317.8
Fat   16.3 g
Cholesterol   102.1 mg
Sodium   141.7 mg
Carbohydrates   2.3 g
Protein   38.7 g

Ingredients

1 1/2 lb. halibut fillets
1/4 C. olive oil
3 garlic cloves, minced
2 tbsp lemon juice
2 tbsp parsley

2 tsp Greek oregano
1/2 tsp salt
1 tsp black pepper

Directions

1. In a bowl, add all the ingredients except the halibut fillets and mix until well combined.
2. Add the halibut fillets and coat with the marinade generously.
3. Place in the fridge for about 1 1/2 hours. Preheat grill.
4. Set your grill for medium-high heat and grease the grill grate.
5. Cook the halibut fillets onto the grill for about 8-10 minutes, flipping once half way through.
6. Enjoy hot.

NEW ENGLAND
Backyard Shrimp

Prep Time: 1 hr 10 mins
Total Time: 1 hr 15 mins

Servings per Recipe: 4
Calories	205.0
Fat	14.6 g
Cholesterol	142.8 mg
Sodium	642.8 mg
Carbohydrates	2.3 g
Protein	15.6 g

Ingredients

1 lb. shrimp, peeled and deveined, tail on
1/4 C. olive oil
3 garlic cloves, mashed
1 tbsp hot shot black and red pepper blend
1/4 tsp ground cumin

cayenne pepper
1/2 lime, juice
salt
1 tbsp chopped parsley

Directions

1. In a bowl, add all the ingredients except the shrimp and mix until well combined.
2. Add the shrimp and coat with the marinade generously.
3. Place in the fridge for about 2 hours.
4. Set your grill for medium-high heat and grease the grill grate.
5. Thread the shrimp onto pre-soaked skewers.
6. Cook them onto the grill for about 2 1/2 minutes, flipping once half way through.
7. Enjoy warm.

Jakarta
Street Food

🥣 Prep Time: 10 mins
🕐 Total Time: 15 mins

Servings per Recipe: 6
Calories   161.3
Fat   6.3 g
Cholesterol   50.3 mg
Sodium   837.9 mg
Carbohydrates   6.6 g
Protein   20.2 g

Ingredients

3 tbsp smooth peanut butter
1/2 C. low sodium soy sauce
1/2 C. lime juice
2 -3 tbsp curry powder
2 garlic cloves, minced

1 tsp hot pepper sauce
4 boneless skinless chicken breast halves, cubed

Directions

1. In a bowl, add all the ingredients except the chicken cubes and mix until well combined.
2. Add the chicken cubes and coat with the marinade generously.
3. Place in the fridge for all the night.
4. Set your grill for high heat and grease the grill grate.
5. Thread the shrimp onto pre-soaked skewers.
6. Cook the skewers onto the grill for about 10 minutes, flipping once half way through.
7. Enjoy warm

STATE FAIR
Lemonade

Prep Time: 5 mins
Total Time: 15 mins

Servings per Recipe: 1
Calories	172.7
Fat	0.2g
Cholesterol	0.0mg
Sodium	10.7mg
Carbohydrates	45.5g
Protein	0.4g

Ingredients

1 1/2 C. lemon juice, seeds and pith removed
1 C. sugar
4 C. cold water
2 lemons, sliced
ice
5 C. pink cotton candy

Directions

1. In a pitcher, add the sugar and lemon juice and mix until dissolves completely.
2. Stir in the lemon slices and cold water and continue stirring until well combined.
3. Divide the lemonade and ice into serving glasses.
4. Add the cotton candy and stir until dissolves completely.
5. Enjoy.

Lemonade
Saint Kitts

🥣 Prep Time: 10 mins
🕐 Total Time: 2 hrs 10 mins

Servings per Recipe: 4
Calories	129.0
Fat	0.3g
Cholesterol	0.0mg
Sodium	6.6mg
Carbohydrates	33.1g
Protein	0.5g

Ingredients

3 C. warm water
2/3 C. lemon juice
1/2 C. sugar
2 tbsp coconut syrup
1/2 C. unsweetened frozen blueberries

1/2 C. frozen red raspberries
1 small star fruit, sliced
ice cube

Directions

1. In a bowl add the sugar, lemon juice, coconut syrup and water and mix until sugar dissolves completely.
2. Cover the bowl and place in the fridge for about 8-20 hours.
3. In a pitcher, add the lemon mixture, berries and star fruit slices and mix.
4. Transfer into ice filled glasses and enjoy.

URBAN
Garden Lemonade

Prep Time: 10 mins
Total Time: 10 mins

Servings per Recipe: 8
Calories	16.9
Fat	0.1g
Cholesterol	0.0mg
Sodium	2.2mg
Carbohydrates	4.1g
Protein	0.7g

Ingredients

3 -4 cucumbers, peeled and chopped

8 -10 mint leaves

1 lemonade

ice cube

Directions

1. In a food processor, add the cucumbers and mint and pulse until smooth.
2. Through a fine mesh strainer, strain the mixture into a bowl, pressing with the back of a wooden spoon.
3. In a pitcher, add the lemonade, cucumber mixture and ice cubes and mix well.
4. Enjoy chilled.

Lebanese
Lemonade

🥣 Prep Time: 5 mins

🕐 Total Time: 5 mins

Servings per Recipe: 1
Calories	87.9
Fat	0.9g
Cholesterol	0.0mg
Sodium	47.6mg
Carbohydrates	25.9g
Protein	1.9g

Ingredients

1 whole organic lemon
1 C. squeezed lemon juice
1 C. agave nectar
1 tbsp of grated ginger

mint leaves
6 - 8 C. of filtered water

Directions

1. In a pot, add the lemon juice and agave and cook until well combined.
2. Remove from the heat and keep aside to cool completely.
3. In a food processor, add the lemon, ginger and agave syrup and pulse until frothy.
4. Add the water and stir to combine.
5. Enjoy with a garnishing of the fresh mint leaves.

BLACK
Lemonade

Prep Time: 30 mins
Total Time: 30 mins

Servings per Recipe: 1
Calories	1297.5
Fat	1.2g
Cholesterol	0.0mg
Sodium	35.7mg
Carbohydrates	337.4g
Protein	2.5g

Ingredients

4 C. water
1 1/2 C. sugar
6 lemons, juice and zest
1/2 C. blackberry

1/2 C. blueberries

Directions

1. In a pan, add the sugar and 2 C. of the water and cook until sugar is dissolved, stirring continuously.
2. Cook for about 4 minutes, stirring frequently.
3. Remove from the heat and stir in the lemon juice, lemon zest and remaining water.
4. Keep aside to cool completely.
5. In a food processor, add both berries and pulse until smooth.
6. Add the berry puree into the lemonade and stir to combine.
7. Keep aside for about 3 hours.
8. Through a strainer, strain the lemonade into pitcher.
9. Refrigerate until chilled completely.
10. Enjoy chilled.

ENJOY THE RECIPES?

KEEP ON COOKING
WITH 6 MORE FREE COOKBOOKS!

Visit our website and simply enter your email address to join the club and receive your 6 cookbooks.

http://booksumo.com/magnet

https://www.instagram.com/booksumopress/

https://www.facebook.com/booksumo/

Made in the USA
Monee, IL
05 May 2020